How to Paint
BOATS AND HARBORS
ALWYN CRAWSHAW

HPBooks

Low Water, Topsham, Devon, 19x14-1/2". Watercolor, private collection.

Published in the United States by
HPBooks
P.O. Box 5367
Tucson, AZ 85703
602/888-2150

Publishers: Bill and Helen Fisher
Executive Editor: Rick Bailey
Editorial Director: Randy Summerlin
Editor: Judith Wesley Allen
Art Director: Don Burton
Book Design: Paul Fitzgerald

©1982 Alwyn Crawshaw
©1983 Fisher Publishing, Inc.
Printed in U.S.A.

First Published 1982 by
Collins Publishers, Glasgow and London

ISBN 0-89586-266-2
Library of Congress Catalog Card Number: 83-80902

CONTENTS

Portrait of an Artist— Alwyn Crawshaw

Alwyn Crawshaw was born in 1934 at Mirfield, Yorkshire, England. He studied at the Hastings School of Art and works in four painting media—watercolors, oils, pastels and acrylics. His favorites are watercolors and acrylics.

Crawshaw is a successful painter, author and lecturer. He is considered a leading authority on acrylic painting. His other books cover landscape painting, watercolors and acrylics in HPBooks' *How to Paint* series.

The author is a fellow of the Royal Society of Arts. He is listed in *Who's Who in Art* and in the fifth edition of *Who's Who in the World.*

Crawshaw paints realistic subjects. Many of his English landscape and harbor scenes have received critical acclaim. He is probably best known for his landscapes. His works have been compared with those of John Constable, the famous English landscape artist.

Crawshaw has always been fascinated by boats and harbors. He has developed this interest further since his move to a home 4 miles from the English coast. His paintings of boats include subjects such as the Henley Royal Regatta, the *Queen Elizabeth 2,* simple fishing boats and humble dinghies.

His most-famous painting of ships probably is *The Silver Jubilee Fleet Review 1977,* shown on pages 12 and 13. The painting commemorates Queen Elizabeth's historic Jubilee celebration.

Crawshaw has discussed his painting techniques on British radio and television. He has been a guest on phone-in programs, talking with callers about their painting problems. He demonstrates his techniques to members of many art societies throughout Britain.

Crawshaw's work became popular after his painting, *Wet and Windy,* was included in the top 10 prints of 1975 by the Fine Art Trade Guild.

Sparkling Water, 20x14-1/2''. Watercolor, collection of Maj. and Mrs. W. Hunter.

His paintings are in private collections throughout the world. His work has been exhibited at the Royal Society of British Artists, London, and in Russia, Poland, Hungary and Romania. He has held one-man shows in Chester and at Harrods department store in London.

One-man exhibitions of his work draw an enthu-siastic audience. The realistic quality of his work makes his scenes seem vaguely familiar.

According to Crawshaw, there are two attributes necessary for artistic success: *dedication* and a *sense of humor.* The need for the first is self-evident. The second "helps you out of many a crisis."

Brittany Sea Mist, 30x20''. Acrylic, private collection.

Painting Boats and Harbors

I have written this book for the student who wants to paint and needs encouragement. It is especially for the person who loves boats.

Painting boats and harbors is an extension of painting landscapes. Unless you are at sea, landscape is part of your picture. It may be cliffs, hills, trees or buildings. The difference is the center of interest: boats. The landscape is in the middle-distance and background. It does not play a big part in your picture.

I did not call this book *marine painting* because that implies ships at sea. Painting the sea is another subject.

Some people say you need to know all about boats to paint them. This is somewhat true. The more we know about a subject, the more natural our paintings are. But you do not need to be a marine architect to enjoy painting boats and harbors!

The more you paint boats, the more you learn about them. You learn as an artist, not as a boat captain. Your key to painting boats realistically is *observation*.

Don't let technical jargon deter you. You don't need a seaman's vocabulary. If you feel better saying "bow" instead of "front" of a boat, go ahead. If you talk with a fisherman and he uses technical words you don't understand, don't bluff. Ask what he means. He'll be pleased to explain terms.

You can paint boats without knowing nautical words, but you'll be more confident if you learn some. Knowing the terminology will not make your painting better. It will make you feel closer to your subject. You'll be less afraid for people to watch you and talk to you while you work. Most important, you'll have *more confidence in yourself and your subject.* A short list of simple technical terms is on page 64.

When you are out painting, listen to seamen talk. Keep an open mind and open eyes to observe and learn.

I had a fascinating chat with a boat owner when I was painting *Three Boats,* which is shown on page 42. I couldn't believe my eyes when I first saw the scene from my car. The muddy moorings and tree-covered hillside coming to the water's edge looked like a boat still life created for me to paint!

I was with my wife. We parked the car and quickly found a good vantage point for painting.

You can work outdoors in almost any medium with a minimum of equipment. I am working in oil paints on the opposite page, in pastels above and in watercolors at right.

After I had worked for an hour and a half, a man appeared from nowhere. People often startle you when you are engrossed in your work. We said "hello" and nothing more. I started talking to him a few minutes later and he seemed pleased to chat. People will often stand and watch because they are afraid to disturb an artist. If *you* feel like talking, make the first move.

This man owned the blue boat I was painting. He told me it was built during World War II and had been a lifeboat on a British cruiser or battleship. It was unseaworthy when he bought it. He had spent hours mending it and getting it shipshape. He used the boat for sea fishing and had been out the day before. The boat on the right in my sketch was a tug that had worked around Dartmouth. The tug and the red boat were being renovated.

I was intrigued by the tunnel above the high-water mark. He said this was an old kiln where lime had been prepared for farms.

I learned one or two nautical terms in our interesting half-hour chat. That conversation made my painting come alive. It gave it meaning beyond an interesting and unusual setting for three boats.

All boats have a story behind them. They are more than planks of wood and pieces of fiberglass or metal.

Unfortunately, we may want to paint at times when it is impossible to get to a big harbor or out to sea. Most of the work in this book concerns small boats and harbors, which are more accessible.

The sketches of large ships at the top of page 41 were done from a fishing harbor wall, looking out to sea. The sketch for the *Queen Elizabeth 2* on pages 56 and 57 was done on a car ferry as my family and I returned from a vacation.

A vacation to the coast gives you the opportunity to paint boats. If you live within driving distance of a coast or river, take a day to sketch and gather information to work from at home.

In a painting, a boat has character. But atmosphere and mood come from the boat's surroundings. A painting without mood or atmosphere is a dead painting. A boat dancing on sunlit water, with strong shadows and twinkling reflections, conveys a happy, carefree, warm mood. If the same boat is in a mist, it loses its color. The reflection is still and the scene is quiet and mysterious.

When you start a painting, decide what type of day it is and how to convey that mood to canvas or paper. The hard part is to keep that mood throughout the painting.

Decide what you are going to paint and let your senses be stimulated by your surroundings. All our senses are with us outside, although our eyes are usually first to experience the scene.

Sense of touch allows us to feel the wind, the warmth of the sun and the sting of ocean spray.

Sense of hearing helps us understand the scene. We hear seagulls scream and perhaps the steady drone of a diesel engine working a water pump or a winch. We hear the wind blowing through rigging lines. In an active fishing harbor, we hear the shouts and greetings as boats come in to unload.

Our sense of smell inspires us to paint boats and harbors. Only at the sea or harbor can you smell salt water, diesel fuel, seaweed and the seamen's catch. A sensitive artist who sees and smells a busy harbor scene can't resist painting it.

Our senses help us paint. When you paint outdoors, let your senses remind you of what you are painting. Your sight gives you the picture. Touch, hearing and smell help you paint the atmosphere. If you feel the sun's warmth, it reminds you that you are painting a warm picture. If you hear seagulls scream, you remain aware the harbor is active.

Painting boat scenes indoors from sketches made outside is a natural way to paint. Most of the old masters worked outside on small studies, using the sketches for inspiration to paint larger paintings indoors. One advantage of painting from a sketch is reflecting on your painting's progress and changing it if you wish.

What is a *sketch?* You have heard artists say, "I did a quick sketch," or "I am going out sketching." What do they mean? Is a sketch a rough drawing or a finished picture? From an artist's point of view, there are four types of sketches:

Enjoyment Sketch—A drawing or painting done on location for enjoyment. The sketch at right is an enjoyment sketch.

Information Sketch—A drawing or painting done to collect information and details to use later.

Atmosphere Sketch—A drawing or painting done to capture atmosphere and mood for use later as atmosphere information. It can be an inspiration sketch for an indoor painting as was the sketch on page 10.

Specific Sketch—A drawing or painting of a *specific place* to gather information, details and atmosphere.

Acrylic paint is an ideal medium for outdoor work.

This is an *enjoyment sketch*.

The sketch conveys the mood or atmosphere of the occasion. It's the basis for a finished studio painting.

All sketches—drawings or paintings—can be *finished* works. Some artists' sketches are preferred to their finished paintings. Sketching is discussed in depth on pages 38-43.

Go out to sketch and paint as much as possible. Observe all you can. When you travel, observe scenes as if you will paint them.

When I was in art school, I was taught to observe and translate what I saw into a mental painting. I still do this.

Carry a small sketchbook whenever you go outdoors. If you have time, draw. Use every opportunity. If you want to sketch, you will find opportunities.

I work in four media—watercolors, oils, acrylics and pastels. To learn more about these media, read these other titles in HPBooks' art series: *How to Paint with Acrylics* and *How to Paint with Watercolors* by Alwyn Crawshaw, *How to Paint with Oils* by Peter John Garrard and *How to Paint with Pastels* by John Blockley. These books cover each medium.

In the following lessons, there is no reason for painting in one medium or another. I may have thought the subject was better suited to that medium.

Try not to become obsessed with your work so you miss the joy of being outside and painting. *Enjoy your painting.*

There will be times when nothing goes right. You will blame everything from your paintbrush to the weather. This happens to all of us. Working from nature is spontaneous. You will always learn, no matter how brief the encounter.

Never throw away a poor sketch or painting. You will often think, "I won't do it this way again!" But you can learn from your mistakes.

In 1977, Queen Elizabeth's Jubilee year, I wanted to paint one of the year's great occasions. I chose the Silver Jubilee Fleet Review at Spithead, off Portsmouth, where the queen reviewed the fleet.

The day's sketches provide an example of a specific sketch. They also clearly show the different uses of the word *sketch*. The fleet review sketches were planned, in contrast to the sketches on page 9 and below.

My wife and I arrived the night before. I checked and rechecked all my painting equipment before we left home. It's better to take too much equipment at a time like this than risk not having enough. Even if you intend to sketch in pencil, take your paints. You may find the circumstances dictate paints for best results.

We stayed near relatives in a hotel by the sea and obtained a first-floor room where I could sketch the review. I was apprehensive about the number of people involved in my sketching plans, but it could not have turned out better.

I planned my sketching carefully. I wanted to paint the fleet illuminated at night, but didn't know if it would be visible on the evening I was there.

Luck was on my side. The family agreed to go see the lights! We left by car at 9:30 p.m., and I took my camera and sketchbook. The road was swarming with people and cars headed for the event. I was excited about painting the illuminated fleet.

The sea looked like a fairyland. The ships were outlined in light. They twinkled and cast a friendly glow over the sea.

I planned to sketch in the light from the car's

This is an *atmosphere sketch*.

headlights. As I walked in front of the car to take a photograph, the ships' lights suddenly went out. I was looking into blackness!

It took me 15 seconds to realize the fleet had turned out its lights. I was bitterly disappointed. But this was not the main event. The thought of the next day kept me going.

We left at 6 a.m. the next morning and walked to where the *Ark Royal* was anchored so I could sketch.

I was excited. I could feel an air of expectancy everywhere. We passed quays where yachts and small boats were preparing to sail, trimmed with bunting and flags. Everyone seemed to have a part in the day's activities, even if only to look.

The sea was even more active. Small service boats went back and forth from ships to shore. Helicopters buzzed around. The *Ark Royal* was majestic with the fleet disappearing out of view behind her. The scene was breathtaking. I wanted to lift it up and take it home to paint.

The cool, early morning wind from the sea brought me back to reality. I sat on a stool and rested the sketchbook on my knees. I used a 2B pencil to sketch.

The sketch is on page 11. I would do my large painting later, but the scene fed my excitement for the rest of the day.

We went to the beach later. I used a low eye level in the sketch shown at the top of page 12. This is a more intimate work than the sketch I did from the hotel that afternoon, which is shown at the top of page 13.

The weather was a problem. The sun came out twice in the morning. This caused a dilemma because the tone of the gray ships made a flat and confusing picture. They needed sunlight to give them form against the gray background of the Isle of Wight.

Under normal circumstances, I would have taken *artistic license* and put sunshine in the picture. Because this was a historical work, I decided that if it rained I would paint the rain. I think the atmosphere of the day was as important as the sights.

After finishing the sketch from the beach, I decided to do the main sketch from the hotel room. I relaxed after I made this decision.

After lunch, I organized my materials in the room. I took some photographs of the fleet.

I sketched with a 2B pencil. You can see from the sketch at the top of page 13 that I used two pages. I used binoculars to read the numbers on the ships' sides. This helped especially with the frigates. I found it difficult to see the subtle differences in the ships because I was so far away.

Compare the morning sketch on page 12 with the afternoon sketch on page 13. The ships are facing in the opposite direction. This confused me when I

My early morning sketch done by the sea.

started the afternoon sketch. I assume it was because the tide turned.

I worked hard on this drawing. I finished just before the royal yacht, *Britannia,* came by with Queen Elizabeth on board. I took three photographs and marked with pencil lines where I would paint the yacht. I could not sketch the yacht. She passed too quickly.

Hundreds of small craft were moored off the fleet, near the beach. Others sailed in the choppy water, with bunting and flags blowing in the wind. Half an hour after the royal yacht passed, the cold, overcast weather turned worse. The Isle of Wight disappeared in the heavy, cold mist.

I felt exhausted that evening. But I had the fantas-

tic feeling I had achieved my goal. The satisfying results were tucked in my sketchbook to work from later.

I was overwhelmed when I began the large 60x20'' canvas. The main problem was to preserve the day's mood. To bring in drama with strong lights and darks would not have conveyed the right atmosphere. I often wonder how different the painting would have looked if the sun had been out.

The photographs were not very good because of the lens I used. However, with my sketches, photographs and *Jane's Fighting Ships* for technical reference, I was happy.

This type of outdoor sketching is different from a normal afternoon's sketch, but it's a good lesson in

The sketch I made at the beach before lunch.

self-discipline and organization. Obviously, you can't wait for another fleet review.

You can find many special boating events. Some are famous national events, while others are small and local. You'll find all of these are fun to paint.

Boating events run on a timetable. Your scene will not wait for you. You must organize yourself around it. If you approach a boating event this way,

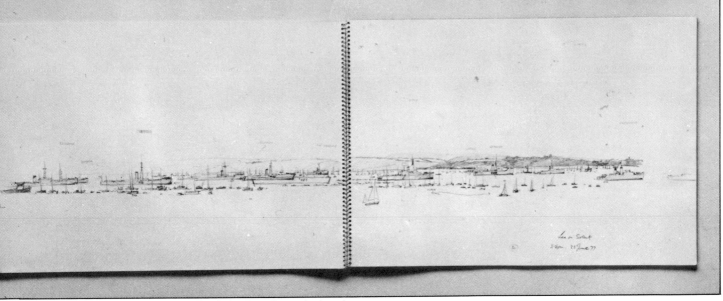

The afternoon sketch of the Fleet Review, done from the hotel.

you'll be better prepared for sketching.

In the following pages, I'll take you through stages of painting. We'll start simply and progress to more advanced painting.

Enjoy the lessons and exercises. If you find some difficult, don't become obsessed with them. Go on to another stage, then come back. A fresh perspective makes a problem easier to solve.

The Silver Jubilee Fleet Review 1977, 60x20". Acrylics, shown by permission of C. Brannon, Yorkshire, England.

Equipment

The equipment you need to paint boats and harbors is the same you need for any subject. You can manage well with the right basics, or you can fill a room with equipment. It's up to you. I suggest you buy the best materials you can afford. You will work more easily with better results.

Materials for acrylic, oil, pastel and watercolor painting are illustrated in the photograph on the opposite page. Basic materials for each of the four media are pictured on pages 16 and 17. These are the essentials. I have used them for the work in this book.

MEDIA

Watercolors—You can buy watercolors in tubes, half pans or whole pans. I don't advise beginners to use tubes. It is more difficult to control the amount of paint on the brush. You can buy pans individually or in boxed selections.

The colors I use are Payne's gray, burnt umber, Hooker's green No. 1, ultramarine blue, alizarin crimson, yellow ochre, cerulean blue, burnt sienna, cadmium red, raw umber, raw sienna and cadmium yellow pale.

Acrylics—I use two types of acrylic paint. One type has a consistency similar to oil paint and is ideal for palette knife work.

The other type of acrylic is better for a brush and takes longer to dry than the first. I used the second type for 99% of the acrylic work in this book. When necessary, you can use texture paste to build up a heavy consistency.

The colors I use are cerulean blue, bright green, burnt umber, raw umber, cadmium yellow, cadmium red, crimson, ultramarine blue, raw sienna and white.

Oils—The oil paints I use are cobalt blue, cadmium red, cadmium yellow, ultramarine blue, viridian, alizarin crimson, burnt umber, yellow ochre and titanium white.

Pastels—There are many pastel colors. Each one comes in several tints ranging from very light-colored tints to dark tints.

The best way to start is to buy a box of artists' soft pastels. When you are accustomed to the medium, buy a larger range of tints.

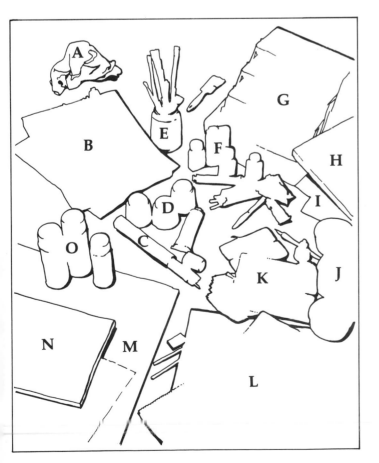

A Paint rag
B Acrylic palette, paints, palette knives
C Brush case and brushes
D Acrylic primer, mediums, texture paste
E Brushes and jar
F Oil-painting varnish, turpentine, drying and impasto mediums, linseed oil, charcoal, tube paints, mixing knife
G Paintbox
H Stretched canvas
I Canvas board
J Water containers
K Watercolor boxes, brushes, sponge, pen and India ink, tissue paper
L Tube watercolors, mixing palette, brushes, pencils, kneaded eraser, watercolor paper, watercolor sketchbook, white designers' gouache
M Pastel papers, sketchbook, dusting brush
N Soft pastels
O Varnish, clear fixative, workable fixative

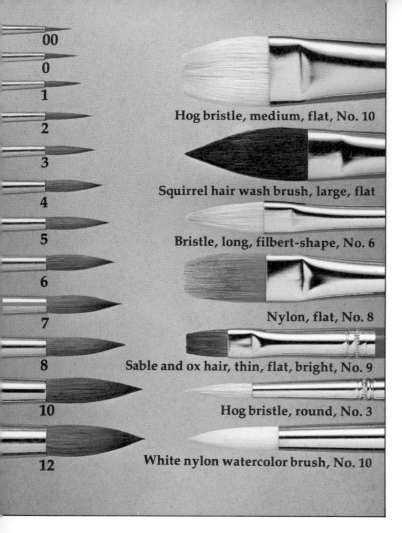

00
0
1
2
3
4
5
6
7
8
10
12

Hog bristle, medium, flat, No. 10

Squirrel hair wash brush, large, flat

Bristle, long, filbert-shape, No. 6

Nylon, flat, No. 8

Sable and ox hair, thin, flat, bright, No. 9

Hog bristle, round, No. 3

White nylon watercolor brush, No. 10

BRUSHES

An artist's most important tool is the brush or painting knife. The brush achieves the painted effects. Whether you want a bold or delicate effect, your brush dictates the result.

It is important to buy the best brushes you can afford. The beginners' basic equipment sets below suggest some of what you need. At left is a selection of brushes showing shapes, sizes and types of bristles. All are actual size. The brushes on the far side are round sable brushes—sizes No. 00 to No. 12. Some brush series have additional sizes, such as Nos. 9, 11 and 14.

Take care of your brushes. This doesn't mean you should keep them in a glass case. A good brush can take a lot of hard work.

BASIC EQUIPMENT SETS

Watercolors—You can start with two brushes: a No. 10 round and a No. 6 round. Quality depends on price, but they should be the best—sable. A paintbox with 12 whole or half pans of color is good for beginners. You also need HB and 2B pencils, a non-

BEGINNERS' BASIC EQUIPMENT SETS

Watercolors

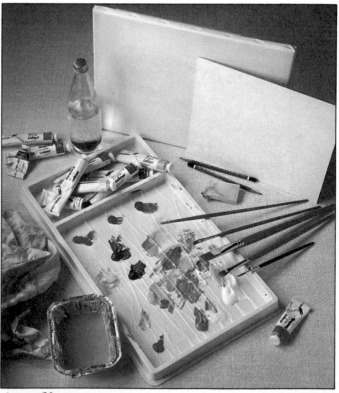

Acrylics

smudging kneaded eraser, a drawing board with watercolor paper or sketchbook, blotting paper, a sponge and a water jar. I suggest you carry a tube of white paint. I use *designers' gouache*—white opaque watercolor.

Acrylics—I use six brushes for exercises in this book. They are Nos. 2, 4, 6 and 12 nylon brushes and a No. 6 round sable brush. For thin lines, I use a No. 1 sable and ox hair brush.

I recommend a palette designed to slow your paint's drying time on the palette and keep it moist. Use a gel retarder to keep the paint wet on the canvas longer.

Use paper, board or canvas for a painting surface. Board and canvas are pictured. An HB pencil, kneaded eraser, paint rag and water jar complete this set.

Oils—You need a box for your paints. The one shown below rests on your knees as an easel. This type of box is sold empty or complete with materials. You can use a small suitcase if you wish.

The brushes are bristle, Nos. 4, 6, 8 and 10, and a round sable No. 6 brush.

You also need a palette knife, purified linseed oil, turpentine, gel medium to speed the paint's drying, canvas board, palette, dippers to hold linseed oil and turpentine, an HB pencil, kneaded eraser and a rag.

Pastels—Use a box of artists' soft pastels. The one pictured below contains 12 colors.

You need paper or a pastel sketchbook with a selection of colored sheets. You also need fixative, a bristle brush to rub out areas of pastel, a kneaded eraser, an HB or 2B pencil and a rag to clean your hands.

There are too many types of paper to discuss here. If you need help finding specific papers, ask someone in an art supply store to help you.

Materials are a matter of choice. Your likes and dislikes will emerge from experience and experimentation.

It's difficult for a beginner to know how to buy the right materials.

All the materials shown here are the best quality. You can buy them in any good art supply store. I hope that with my suggestions you won't worry too much about what to get. If you are still unsure, take this book along and you won't have any problems!

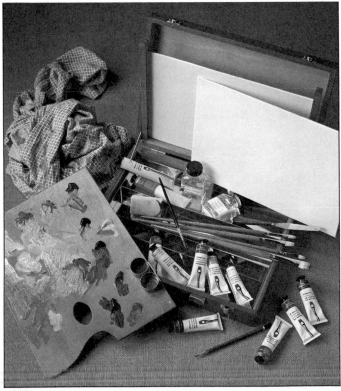

Oils

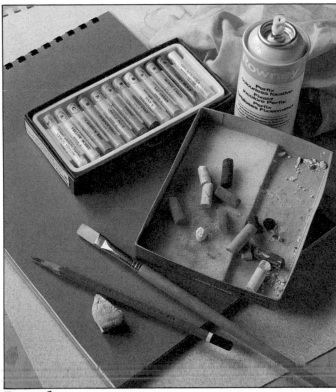

Pastels

Basic Drawing & Perspective

A drawing is the basis for a painting. It is the guide to what you want to paint.

You can use pencil for watercolor and pastel, and charcoal or paint for oil and acrylic painting. I use pencil. Personal preference dictates what you use. You will find your own method as you practice and gain confidence.

If you are a beginner, I suggest you follow my instructions carefully at first. If my way is comfortable for you, then keep using my methods. If you later adopt other methods, let it happen. You won't break any rules.

I am often asked, "Must I be able to draw to paint pictures?" The answer is "no," but you must have a simple, basic knowledge of *perspective*. Perspective drawing is a technique that gives a three-dimensional appearance to the shapes and forms of objects.

If you want accurate details in a picture, you need more drawing ability. Details can be suggested, or you can paint general impressions. This does not call for precise drawing skills.

There are some basic rules of perspective. Become familiar with the terms *horizon, eye level* and *vanishing point.* How do these relate to drawing?

The *horizon* is always at *eye level* when you look out to sea, even if you climb a cliff or lie flat on the sand. Standing outdoors, hold a pencil horizontally at arm's length in front of your eyes. The pencil is always on the horizon. So the horizon and the eye level are the same.

If you are in a room, there is no horizon, but you still have an eye level. Do the same pencil exercise. Your eye level is where the pencil crosses the opposite wall.

If two parallel lines on the ground are extended to the horizon, they come together at the *vanishing point.* Railroad lines appear to get closer until they meet in the distance. The meeting point is at the vanishing point.

On the opposite page, I drew an orange rectangle, box A, and a line above it to show the eye level. At the left end of the eye-level line I made a mark—the vanishing point (VP). This point can be anywhere on the horizon line. With a ruler, I drew a line from each corner of the rectangle to the vanishing point. This created the two sides, bottom and top of the box.

To create the other end of the box, I drew a rectangle parallel with the front of the box and inside the vanishing point guidelines. This is a "transparent" box drawn in perspective.

Practice this exercise. Move the eye level up and down. Change the shape of the box. If you turn the book upside down, you see the box with a low eye level.

DRAW A SIMPLE BOAT

Box B is slightly changed. Draw a line from the top left corner of the orange rectangle to the bottom right corner. Do the same with the other two corners. The midpoint of the rectangle is where the lines cross.

You can find this midpoint with a ruler if you are looking at the rectangle straight-on. But if the rectangle is at an angle—drawn in perspective, as in box C—you can't use a ruler.

Next, draw a vertical line parallel to the sides of box B, crossing the midpoint. Mark a vanishing point on the horizon line. Draw two lines from the vanishing point to the top and bottom of your central vertical line. You have divided the box into two equal halves as seen in perspective. Draw a line parallel to the top orange line, farther back on the vanishing point guidelines. Where it meets the edges, draw parallel lines to the bottom guidelines.

From these points, draw four lines. Two will meet at the top of the front vertical line and two at the bottom of the vertical line. Follow the drawing and you will find it simple. You have drawn a simplified version of a boat's bow. If all boats and ships were made this simply, our lesson would stop here. But we have to go further.

The orange rectangles in boxes C and D are drawn at an angle in perspective. You have two vanishing points, one on the left and one on the right. Follow the steps in boxes A and B again. In box D, I narrowed the boat's stern and cut away part of the deck by using the two vanishing points.

In box E, I drew a bird's-eye-view. In box F, I added a realistic shape to the ship. In box G, I drew a small cargo vessel to show how to draw the superstructure. These exercises show how to use simple perspective to draw objects that have basic cube shapes.

How do you use perspective when you paint? Draw your picture *freehand*—as you see it. Correct it with mechanical perspective if it looks wrong. To work out your boat perspective, use the boat's main straight lines as sides of the box. Don't be confused by the boat's subtle curves. You can refine the curves after you have drawn the basic cube shape.

Finally, practice perspective on paper. You will enjoy it and find that a boat becomes less difficult to draw.

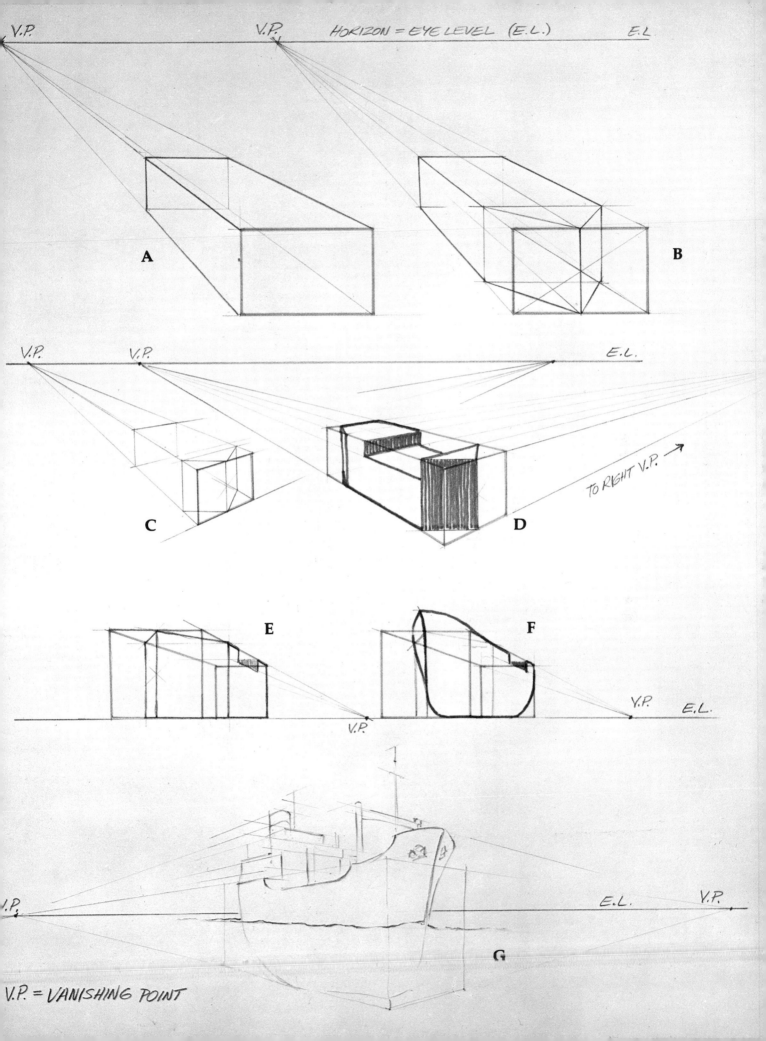

V.P.   V.P.   HORIZON = EYE LEVEL (E.L.)   E.L

A

B

V.P.   V.P.   E.L.

C

D

TO RIGHT V.P.

E

F

V.P.

Y.P.   E.L

V.P.

V.P.   E.L.   V.P.

G

V.P. = VANISHING POINT

Start Painting

EXPERIMENTING WITH PAINT

Now you can start painting. You must first choose a medium. Oils may be too messy for you and watercolors too unpredictable. Quick-drying acrylics may be too difficult to cope with, or pastels too dusty. Whatever medium you use, you will have to master its peculiarities to enjoy it.

I suggest you start with watercolors. Most people used water-based paint as children. We dipped a brush in water and mixed it with paint. This is a basic method of watercolor painting.

Watercolor is also economical. The equipment is easy to carry.

Many beginners find it difficult to start painting. This is natural. From the first brushstroke, the painting is a creation. At first, beginners tend to be sensitive to criticism of their work.

You can't run before you walk, so let's start doodling and experimenting with paint. Get some paper and brush the paint on it. See how the brushes handle. Add more water to your watercolor paint. Use less water. Try anything you like to become familiar with the medium.

You will end up with an odd-looking, painted paper. But you will understand the paint's application much better!

Practice with the medium you choose before you try to mix colors. Below are my doodles in watercolors and oils. Don't worry about how they look. They are nothing more than experiments.

MIXING COLORS

You will find it exciting to create colors. Hundreds of colors exist around us, but there are only three basic colors: red, yellow and blue. These are called *primary colors*. They are pictured at top right.

All other colors and shades of colors are a combination of these. We use different reds, yellows and blues to re-create nature's colors. The top two rows at right show two samples of each primary color.

In the bottom three rows, I have mixed the primary colors. Cadmium yellow mixed with cadmium red makes orange. To make the orange more yellow, add more yellow than red, and vice versa. Add white (not shown) to make the orange lighter.

Cadmium yellow mixed with ultramarine blue makes green. If you add white, you get light green.

My lists of paint colors on page 15 do not include black. Some artists use black. I don't. I believe it is a "dead" color—too flat. I mix black from the primary colors, as in the bottom row at right. You may find it difficult to get really dark colors at first. If you get frustrated, try a premixed black—but use it sparingly.

If you want a color to be "cooler," add blue. If you want it "warmer," add red.

Now, you must practice mixing colors.

Do your mixing on your palette with a brush. Paint daubs on paper or canvas. Don't worry about shapes. You are concerned with colors. Experimentation and practice are the only guidelines you have. Select a colorful object and try to imagine what colors you would mix to obtain it.

There are only three basic colors. The amount to use of each one is the most important part of mixing a color. You can easily mix green as we did at right. But if it is to be a yellow-green, you have to experiment on your palette. You must add yellow until you have the color you want. Mixing colors is an art you must practice and improve on.

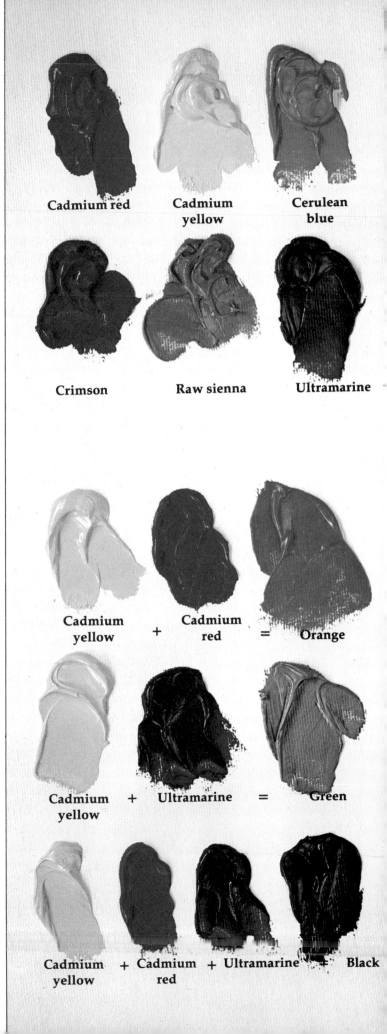

Cadmium red   Cadmium yellow   Cerulean blue

Crimson   Raw sienna   Ultramarine

Cadmium yellow + Cadmium red = Orange

Cadmium yellow + Ultramarine = Green

Cadmium yellow + Cadmium red + Ultramarine + Black

Painting the Sky

If you are confident about mixing colors, you are ready to start simple exercises. You won't be able to mix every color you want yet. This takes time and practice. Working on exercises or simple paintings gives you more inspiration than mixing colors and painting funny shapes!

These exercises are simple. Don't try to put too many details in them. If you think I have put in too many details, finish your exercise when you have gone as far as you can.

Repeat the exercises often. They are meant to help you develop confidence in painting. Copying my exercises from the book will increase your knowledge of the subject matter. You will be more familiar with it when painting outdoors.

I said earlier that you must be familiar with your paints, brushes and color mixing. The subject matter is just as important. Confidence comes from being familiar with your work. A good painting shows confidence and knowledge of the subject.

I think the most important part of any outdoor painting is the sky, so I have chosen the sky as your first subject. My comments refer to the sky generally and can be used with any medium. If I paint an exercise in watercolors, and you are working in oils, try it in your medium.

The sky is important because it determines the at-mosphere of the painting. No matter what the scene, the sky conveys the type of day—sunny, rainy, windy or cold.

If you were painting a busy harbor on a sunny day, there might be fishermen with no shirts on. Sunlight would dance on the water and passers-by might stroll in brightly colored clothes. The mood and atmosphere come from the busy harbor activities. But the weather affects every element, and the sky depicts the weather. If you capture the day's mood in your sky, it should follow through in the painting. The sky reminds you of the mood as you paint.

When you are ready to work outside, put paints aside. Use a 2B or 3B pencil and have a kneaded eraser handy. Keep a sketchbook just for skies. It will become a valuable source of information.

Look at the sky for a while and watch the pattern of movement. Observe the changing cloud formations. Half-close your eyes to see the sky in simple blocks of light and dark color. Soon you will have the feel of the sky and be ready to draw it.

Start in the middle of your paper, so you have room to work in any direction. Roughly draw the shapes of the main cloud formations. Add form by shading with your pencil.

The sky changes constantly. If you have observed

cloud formations and movement, you should be able to put the design and mood on paper. Don't try to copy every cloud. Aim for an *impression* of the sky. Note the sun's position, time of day, type of day and date on your sketches. Don't make these sketches larger than 8x11''. You may even work as small as 4x5''.

When you have practiced drawing the sky, try it with paint. The approach is the same. Use only three or four colors at first. Add land or sea to the sketch to give depth and dimension to the sky. Try it with pastels. They are good for fast-moving skies. You can color large areas quickly and sensitively.

SIMPLE EXERCISES

The sky at the bottom of the opposite page, shown in two stages, is pastel on a small piece of gray paper. Work yellow ochre up from the horizon. Follow it with burnt umber, applying it over the first color. In the same way, work indigo up to the top of the sky. Paint the sea with the same color. Put in clouds with short, sharp strokes of cobalt blue. Finally, add the boat with a creamy shade of white.

At top right is a watercolor done in three colors. They were mixed with plenty of water to get different shades. I used 140-pound, cold-pressed watercolor paper, 8x5''.

Wet the paper with clean water. While it is wet, paint the first stage with a No. 10 sable brush. Paint the clouds with a No. 6 sable brush. When the first clouds are dry, paint a darker cloud over them with a darker mix of the same colors. Put in the hills and boats with a stronger mix of these colors. Practice this type of small watercolor sky. Create different moods and effects. Use various papers, from common writing paper to watercolor papers.

The painting of a sun in the mist at bottom right is oil paint on oil-primed canvas, 8x5-1/2''. To simplify color mixing, I used three colors and white.

Work from the sun outward, using a No. 6 bristle brush. Next, work cobalt blue from the sides in, mixing it with the sun's colors. Use circular brushstrokes. Paint the boat with a No. 6 sable.

This is another simple sky. Copy it, and then experiment with other sky effects in oils.

Remember this guideline: *The sky sets the mood of every painting.*

Payne's gray
Yellow ochre
Alizarin crimson

Titanium white
Yellow ochre
Cadmium red

Add Cobalt blue

Painting Water

I am fascinated by water, probably because I love to fish.

I formerly lived on the southern coast of England. I fished the sea in a small boat. Between bouts of seasickness and attention to my fishing rod, I observed and sketched the sea.

The fascination of water, like the sky, is its changing mood. Its appearance depends on many factors. Prevailing weather conditions give water its visual mood. Changing reflections, such as those of moving boats, constantly alter its look.

Water is exciting to paint. It is not difficult to master if you are careful. As with the sky, the secret is to observe and simplify shapes and colors.

Students are always mystified about the color of water. The color usually depends on surroundings reflected in the water. Water can be self-colored, as in a muddy inlet. Colors of reflections are slightly darker than the reflected object. Reflections are fainter—and eventually nonexistent—as you get farther from the object.

Look at the sketch of the large ships at the top of page 41. There is no reflection. They were about 1-1/4 miles from me, and I could not see a reflection. The boats at the bottom of page 41 were closer and showed more reflections.

Paint water the same way you did sky. Copy my exercises first. When you feel confident, go out and sketch. Use a 3B pencil and the same size sketchbook you used for the sky. Eventually you will find a size you prefer for sketching. You will do best if you stick to this size.

Find some still water with good reflections. Sit down, relax and look at the water. Concentrate on those reflections. Half-close your eyes. The reflections will appear clearer and more defined, because you see only the dark and light colors.

Sketch the shapes of the reflections with your 3B pencil. Put in highlights by taking off some of the pencil with horizontal strokes of your kneaded eraser. You can use this method to show ripples.

Next, find moving water to draw. As with still water, observe the reflections. Your eyes will move with the water and the reflections will change. The secret is to fix your gaze on one spot on the water. Don't let the movement take your eyes with it. As you see, reflections actually stay in one place. They may move a little with water ripples, but they stay in the same location. Water movement is shown in floating debris, water plants and reflected light.

Half-close your eyes again. Fix your gaze on one spot, identify the reflections and movement. Then start your sketch. Don't fall into the trap of drawing or painting horizontal strokes all over your water. If you put in too many, it looks artificial and contrived. Use horizontal lines to define water movement or reflected light only where necessary.

Never overwork water in a painting. In watercolors or pastels, you can leave some paper unpainted to represent water. In oils or acrylics, use your paint

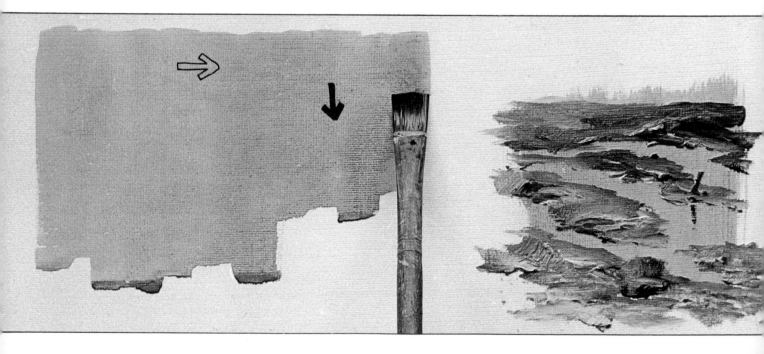

thinly, but thicken it for water movement or highlights.

Water with no reflections is easy to see in person. But when you paint, water without reflections can be hard to portray. Solve this by adding reflections of your own. Water left in mudholes as the tide recedes could have driftwood or an old anchor reflected in it. Use your imagination when nature lets you down and leaves you with flat-looking, uninteresting water.

The photograph at the bottom of the opposite page has two arrows. One is black and the other is outlined. I will use arrows like these in the book to explain how the brush moves. The black arrow shows the direction of the brushstroke. The outlined arrow shows the direction in which you are painting on the paper. The photograph shows the brush moving to the right after each downward stroke.

Both exercises on the opposite page show how to give the impression of water with acrylic paints. First paint the water as you would a watercolor wash—very wet. Paint in downward strokes. When it is dry, paint the mud around it.

SIMPLE EXERCISES

Overpainting water is a big pitfall. The distinction between water and reflection is lost. *Simplify shapes.* In the sketch at top right I simplified the painting so the white watercolor paper represents water. Only the reflections are painted.

Do this exercise and try your own reflections. Use 6x5'' watercolor paper and a No. 6 sable brush. Paint the pilings with Payne's gray and Hooker's green No. 1. Paint the boat with a mix of cadmium yellow pale and alizarin crimson. For the shadows, use darker shades of the pilings' colors—more paint, less water.

Before you paint reflections, relax the tension in your wrist and fingers. Practice on scrap paper. Paint the reflections with a watery mix of the pilings' colors. Don't try to copy mine. You will lose the freedom of line you need to represent reflections. Relaxed brushstrokes help create the impression of reflections.

The paintings in oils at lower right are more complicated. We have to paint water with no reflections.

First, paint the pier with the colors shown. Vary the amount of each color to produce different wood tones. Paint the blue water. Now use the pier colors to paint reflections, as you did in the previous exercise. Then paint among your reflections with a mix of all the colors. Use plenty of titanium white and cobalt blue.

Let your paint mix with reflections in places. Use thicker paint in the lighter areas. This exercise was painted on a canvas board, 8x5-1/2'', with a No. 6 bristle brush.

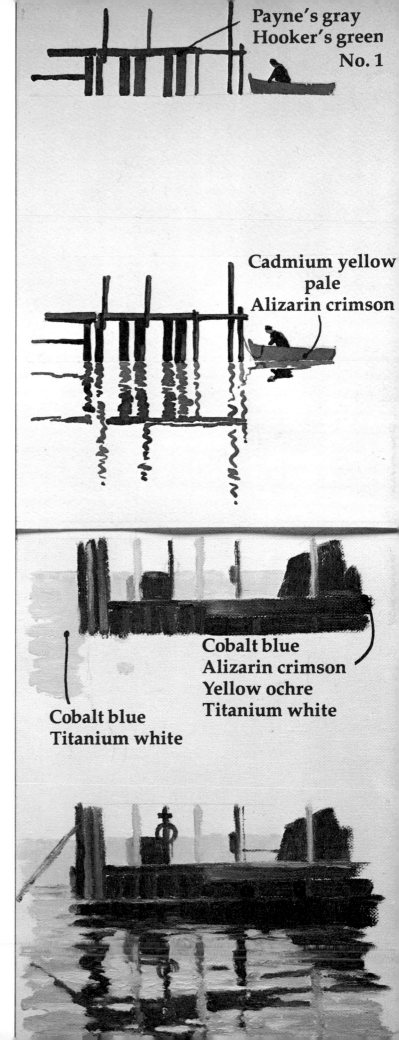

Payne's gray
Hooker's green
No. 1

Cadmium yellow
pale
Alizarin crimson

Cobalt blue
Alizarin crimson
Yellow ochre
Titanium white

Cobalt blue
Titanium white

Painting Boats

Now it's time to paint boats.

When you start, don't put in too many details. Keep the boats simple. Concentrate on their shape and form.

Perhaps you've heard the joke where someone shows a piece of white paper and says, "That's a white cat in a snowstorm." Of course, you would not expect to see anything. But if you did see a white cat in a snowstorm, you could make out shapes and forms because of light and shade. There would be *variations* of white—some light, some dark.

If there is no light, you can't see form. Think of a sunset just before dark. If you look at buildings and boats against the sky, they are in silhouette. They merge into each other and form strange, dark, unreal shapes. This is because they have no light on them. Light creates form—three-dimensional shape. This is exaggerated when the sun is out. It casts strong shadows. You see light against dark, and the shapes contrast.

Half-close your eyes and look at the clouds. You will not see much contrast between the grays on white clouds. You will get a better impression of form because only the lights and darks are visible. The darks are darker and the lights are lighter. Use this method to observe all subjects.

After your earlier work on drawing and perspective, your artistic awareness of boats should be sharper. These exercises should be easier. Don't worry about details. If you worry and fuss over them, you will think boats are too difficult to paint.

Relax and enjoy these exercises. If you get stuck on an exercise, try another one you find easier.

SIMPLE EXERCISES

In the painting below, I used three acrylic colors, plus white, and a No. 4 nylon brush. Follow my painting. If you think there are too many details, leave some out.

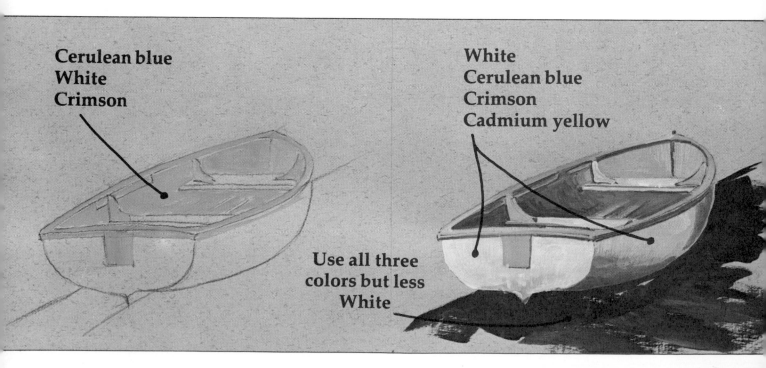

Cerulean blue
White
Crimson

White
Cerulean blue
Crimson
Cadmium yellow

Use all three colors but less White

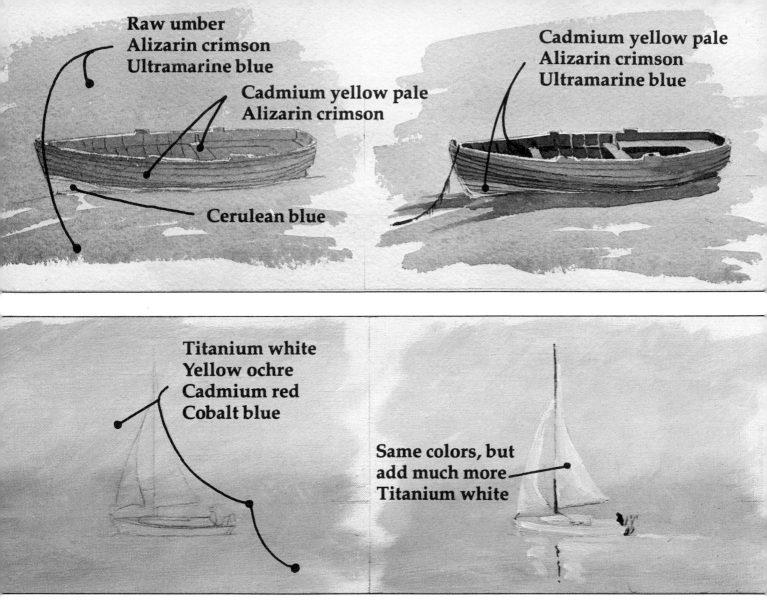

Raw umber
Alizarin crimson
Ultramarine blue

Cadmium yellow pale
Alizarin crimson

Cerulean blue

Cadmium yellow pale
Alizarin crimson
Ultramarine blue

Titanium white
Yellow ochre
Cadmium red
Cobalt blue

Same colors, but
add much more
Titanium white

The exercise at the top of the page is a watercolor. The colors are applied with single washes of color. Use a No. 10 sable brush and paint the background first, then the boat and the blue at the bottom. Use the same colors—but darker—and your No. 6 sable brush to put in shadows inside the boat and outside the hull. Finish with a shadow on the mud.

The second exercise above is on oil-primed canvas. I used three colors and white. Start at the top of the sky and work down, varying the amount of each color as you go. Paint the boat with thicker paint and add plenty of titanium white. Paint the boat while the sky and sea are still wet. Pull some of the sky color into the sail area. This helps create the shadow areas. Use a No. 6 sable brush for the mast and man, a No. 8 bristle brush for the sky and a No. 4 bristle brush for the boat.

The exercise on the next page is also on oil-primed canvas with oil color. It is painted in three colors and white. Note that the red is alizarin crimson, not cadmium red. This sailing barge is

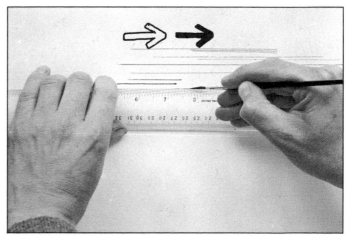

Use this method to paint rigging lines or straight edges in watercolors or acrylics. For wet oils, lay the ruler on the canvas edge. I prefer a transparent ruler so I can see through to the painting. The secret to making straight lines is to let the *ferrule*, or metal part of the brush, run against the edge of the ruler. Work from left to right if you are right-handed, and vice versa. To ensure a steady hand, hold your breath when you make the brushstroke. This helps prevent unwanted hand movement.

Cobalt blue
Alizarin crimson
Yellow ochre
Titanium white

Yellow ochre
Alizarin crimson
Titanium white

Add a little Cobalt blue
for shadows

Cobalt blue
Alizarin crimson

more difficult than the previous exercises.

I omitted the barge rigging to make it simpler. I haven't painted many details. Use your No. 8 bristle brush and start with the blue sky, working down to the horizon. Paint the sails and barge hull with your No. 4 bristle brush. Paint the water, reflections and the darker areas on the sails. Darken the hull and put in any details with your No. 6 sable.

In the left exercise on the opposite page, I used three acrylic colors plus white. I have left dark-gray paper to represent water. We also did this in the water exercise when we used white paper for water and added reflections. The only difference is the paper color, which is ideal for this wintry scene.

Paint the sky and land to the water's edge with a No. 6 nylon brush. Use sky colors for the land, but with much less white. Paint the smaller brown boat with a No. 6 sable and the white boat with a No. 4 nylon brush. If you find the No. 6 too large for details, try a smaller brush—Nos. 3 or 4.

Paint the nearest boat with a No. 6 sable brush. Then paint the gray snow on the two brown boats and the mast and shadow on the white boat. Paint the other side of the scene with your No. 6 sable brush. Use dark colors first and add light colors to represent snow. Details are only *suggested*. They are painted freely.

Use your No. 6 nylon brush to paint the mud and snow in the foreground. Add snow highlights and other details on the boats and mud. If you want the paint to work easier on this paper, add a little *gel retarder* to your paint. Gel retarder makes acrylic paint dry slower, which gives you more time to work the paint.

The exercise at far right has a little more work in it. I painted it in acrylics while my brushes were still wet from the last exercise!

Use your No. 6 nylon brush for everything except detail work. I kept the boat's hull simple. There is little shading or blending of colors. Don't copy the water exactly from mine, but use my painting as a guide. Notice how paper represents sky this time, not water.

If you can do this exercise confidently, and are happy with the results, you have come a long way. This is a turning point. You should be relaxed and confident about your work by now. If necessary, go back to the earlier exercises and practice more. Practice simply means to paint. Paint more and you will get better and enjoy it more.

Now we will use pen and pastel. The exercise on page 30 is done on paper. Use a drawing pen with black ink and three pastel colors.

Draw the barges and small boats with an HB pencil. You don't need details—just enough to follow with a pen. The pen suggests details, so don't try to put in everything. You want an *impression* of rigging, masts and sails. If you were drawing the

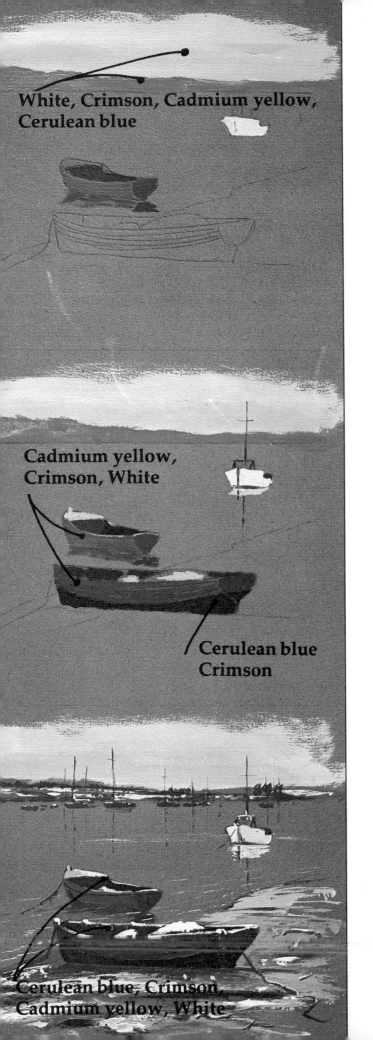

White, Crimson, Cadmium yellow,
Cerulean blue

Cadmium yellow,
Crimson, White

Cerulean blue
Crimson

Cerulean blue, Crimson,
Cadmium yellow, White

Cerulean blue
White
Crimson

Cerulean blue
Crimson
Cadmium yellow
White

Crimson
Cadmium yellow
Cerulean blue
White

White
Cadmium yellow

All three colors
but less White

Yellow ochre

Pen and black ink

Burnt umber

Cadmium red

barges from a distance, you could not see all the rigging. You would see only shapes.

Paint the sky with yellow ochre. Smudge some pastel with your finger on the sail area. Paint the sails and their reflections with burnt umber. Use cadmium red to paint the barge bottoms. Paint the sea behind the barges with yellow ochre.

The pastel covers some of your pen work, but don't worry. Brush off the excess pastel with a small, damp sable brush. Your pen line will show again. Leave some pen covered. This adds to your painting's character. Finish with pen, adding any details you want.

The simplified boat exercise in watercolor on the opposite page is more complicated. Details are suggested by a pen with black ink. This technique is called *pen and wash*. It doesn't matter whether you use pen before or after the paint.

In this case, watercolor is used first over an HB-pencil drawing. I used 140-pound, cold-pressed watercolor paper. Paint the sky with your No. 10 sable brush. Use cerulean blue, yellow ochre and alizarin crimson mixed with plenty of water. Paint the background buildings with your No. 6 sable brush and a mixture of ultramarine blue, alizarin crimson and yellow ochre.

Paint the dock with Payne's gray, yellow ochre and alizarin crimson. Paint the deck with yellow ochre, and the hull and smokestack with Payne's gray, ultramarine blue and yellow ochre.

Put details on the ship's superstructure with your No. 6 sable brush. Use the dark colors you have already mixed. Darken the hull with the same colors you used before, but use more paint. Use cerulean blue, alizarin crimson and yellow ochre for the water. Paint the ship with Payne's gray and alizarin crimson. When the paint has dried, work over it with a pen. Suggest as many or as few details as you want.

When you paint boats, don't worry too much about technical correctness. If you paint a detailed, close-up view of a boat or ship, you have to be technically correct for your painting to look right. If you paint an impression of the same boat, your painting shows what you see in shape and form. This is not necessarily technically correct.

Painting Harbor Details

The harbor is usually the background for a boat picture. Next time you sketch in a harbor, concentrate on details—close-ups of harbor fixtures and fittings. You can use these as information sketches when you paint at home.

Most objects at a harbor, such as anchors or fishing nets, are related to boats, but some are not obvious. I once saw a trash can at the entrance to a yacht harbor. If I had not noticed it, I would never have put it into a painting. The same is true of the gas pumps on the opposite page. Until you *see,* you don't realize that mundane objects are necessary in a harbor scene.

Each type of harbor has its own character. A fishing harbor has nets, lobster pots and seagulls. A yacht harbor has a different atmosphere. The activity is for pleasure as much as work.

Docks are different. They deal with cargo from large ships. If docks are accessible and you like large subjects, you will be in your element painting large cargo ships, cranes and warehouses.

The sketches opposite and below are a small portion of the harbor details I have sketched. Make a habit of doing an information sketch of the harbor every time you finish a sketch or painting on location. It may take only 10 minutes, depending on the subject, and will discipline you not to focus all your attention on the boats.

Always ask permission to paint in a certain spot in a harbor. Nine times out of 10 you can. It is embarrassing and wastes time to start work and be asked to move.

Painting from Photographs

I believe photographs can help students and professional artists. However, *photographs should not replace painting on location. They should be used only as a secondary reference.* Photographs should not be a shortcut to your personal observation and experience outdoors.

Artists use electric lights, tube paints, plastic palettes, nylon brushes and acrylic paints without a second thought. All these items come through modern technology. Yet people are not as afraid of them as they are of the camera.

Despite the trend to scorn it, perhaps many artists *do* use the camera. It can be an invaluable painting aid. Imagine asking John Constable, when he was out sketching, "Would you like to take back that scene and look at it any time on your own studio wall?" Would he refuse?

Once we accept the camera as a working tool for the artist, we have to assess how to use it. You can buy a complicated camera and take a course in photography. Then you need years of experience to achieve perfect results. By then you are a good photographer but have forgotten about painting!

Concentrate on painting, not the camera. Use a simple camera that does most of the work for you. I use a 35mm camera, but any type will do. All you want is a snapshot for *reference*. These are my ways of using photographs. You may develop your own.

Taking your own photographs helps you experience the scene with your senses. This is important. When you see the photograph later at home, it triggers your memory. You are back at the scene, smelling, hearing and feeling it.

I recommend taking slides instead of prints. You can project the image any size you like, sit in front of it and get into the mood. It is difficult to recapture a mood from a small print. The larger you project the image, the more details you see. This is important for painting boats.

I photograph for information and atmosphere. When sketching, I take a photograph and then forget about the camera. I know I will see the scene again when the film is developed.

I paint the picture from my sketching notes.

When the photographs come back, I check details and add or subtract if necessary. If the painting has complicated details, or if I am recording a special occasion, I do not start the finished painting until I have the photographs.

If you use photographs this way, you are not copying. You use them as memory triggers for details. Photographs are for reference only. *You create on canvas your own experience—not the camera's.*

If you photograph what you sketch, you will notice a difference between middle-distance objects and distant objects. Distant images look farther away in the photograph than in your sketch, and those in the middle-distance do also. Apart from technical reasons, this is because the camera sees everything, but *you see only what you want to see.* This is why every artist's picture is different, even of the same view.

The photograph at the top of the opposite page was taken before I made the sketch below it. The inset photograph shows me sketching the scene. See how the middle-distance appears farther away in the photograph? In the sketch, the inn across the river looks closer than in the photograph. The trees play a more important part in the sketch.

These are typical of sketches and photographs from which I paint larger pictures. I use the proportions and composition, or design, from the sketch. I use the photograph for reference and as a guide to the local colors.

I asked an old boatman about the little boat. The man dressed in red is an eel catcher. The net in the boat is an eel trap. The man sets the traps at night, which explains the old oil lamp on the mast. I could not figure out its purpose. The man in the dinghy on the left of my sketch is the eel man going off for lunch. Yes, I put the same man in my sketch twice!

Students often ask me timidly, "May I use photographs?" They look around quickly to see if their fellow students have heard. This confusion about photographs should be dispelled. It is not a crime to use them. Use them correctly and don't be ashamed to admit it.

This is my photograph of the eel man. The inset shows me sketching.

Below is my pencil sketch of the eel man. The dimensions are 16-1/2x11-1/2''.

Painting from Memory

Everyone sometimes paints from memory or imagination. When we were children, we drew trees, boats, the sea and birds from memory. None of these subjects were visible at the time. Working from memory is a natural way to paint or draw. Most of us doodle on the phone or in a meeting. Those doodles are anything from scribbled lines to little drawings.

We can't draw from memory without seeing an object first. We sketch from nature to observe and collect information. That information is in our memory when we want to paint at home.

Imagination is different. If you paint a boat from another world, as artists do who illustrate science fiction books—this comes partly from your imagination. You need your memory for information and your imagination to create and add spice to your picture.

Some people have better memories than others. If you find it difficult to remember scenes, try to cultivate your visual memory. Sketching is one of the best ways to do this. Sketching teaches you to observe—to *look* and *see*. We normally see only what we want to see.

If you looked at a harbor scene for 10 minutes, you would probably remember only obvious details. You would remember the restaurant on the other side of the harbor wall and the shop next to your parked car. You might miss the big, red boat that was in front of you—it was in your way and you moved to one side of it to see where the children were. You were interested in the restaurant and shop. Your visual memory was "blind" to the rest of the harbor.

If you later draw the harbor at home, you remember what you wanted to see—a picture. Next time you are out, try to see places as paintings. The more you sketch, the more you look at scenes as paintings and remember them.

This practice lets you control your working conditions. You decide what to paint, what mood of nature you want to portray and what your working conditions will be at home. This is the ideal way to work in winter when it is difficult to get out.

Unfortunately, we are restricted in regard to accurate details when we paint like this. Landscapes are easier to paint this way than boat scenes. If a tree branch is too high or too low, no one can tell. If a mast is positioned incorrectly on a yacht, it is evident immediately. The details in a harbor scene are too much to re-create from memory, even with a vivid imagination.

There are two ways around this problem. First, use sketches as reference for details. Then create your picture from memory. Your photographs show details. Add information from your sketches, and add extra details from your imagination.

The alternative is to paint without many details. Position your nearest boat or building in the middle-distance or background. It will be too far away to need details. Concentrate on the scene's atmosphere. Your sky is important. Your foreground can be of a general nature, such as water or mud.

When painting from memory, the sky gives you the same freedom a tree does in a landscape. A cloud can be too thick, long, short or dark, and it won't matter for accuracy. The foreground of water or mud can be empty of boats or debris. Boats and buildings do not need many details because they are in the middle-distance. Sunsets and early morning paintings are perfect for this because boats are silhouetted against the sky. You can't see details in silhouettes.

I have a method for painting from memory. You will develop your own method.

I draw the proportions of the finished painting on my sketchbook. Usually I work half the size of the finished painting. I sit in front of the canvas or paper on which I will paint. This gives me a feel for the finished size on which I will work later.

I relax and imagine different moods of nature. These come from memories of different days I have experienced—not necessarily painting. Our memories are full of these visions. Depending on your mood, a recollection will surface. If you find it difficult, look at your sketches or family photographs. These can trigger a memory of mood and atmosphere.

A good day's work behind you, or a bad day with the boss or children, brings different memories to

Top: My pencil sketch, 7-3/4x3-1/2'', is drawn from memory and imagination. Above: This is the watercolor-and-pen painting, 15-1/2x7'', that resulted from the sketch.

mind. A good day is likely to bring peaceful memories. A not-so-good day may stir visions of rough seas and wind-swept harbors.

Start the sketch when you have a vision in mind. Capturing a mood of nature gives life to a painting. Without it, a painting is dull.

Next, decide on the picture's content. This can easily come from the scene that you recalled. If not, focus on the mood and create a picture around it. If your mood is of a windy, rainy day, use dramatic lines and shapes to give movement. A yacht with sails billowing or an inland waterway with wind-whipped waves and storm clouds coming up are examples. Practice this throughout your painting career.

Then draw the scene in a sketchbook, not on the canvas or paper for the finished painting. If your picture changes after your sketch, don't worry. You create it any way you want. This method of painting gives you total control over your subject and painting conditions. I love to paint this way. You won't be disappointed when you try it.

Outdoor Pencil Sketching

Before we start step-by-step exercises, we must consider the reasons and requirements for sketching outdoors.

First, you must work from nature to understand it. Boats and harbors are outdoors, not indoors. This doesn't mean you can paint only outside. I do many paintings indoors, but information and inspiration come from sketching on location.

You may find it difficult to sketch outside as much as you like. If so, do as much as possible when you have the opportunity. Save time by doing small sketches. If you like to paint in color from pencil sketches, then do more pencil sketches on location. They can be done quicker than a painting.

A pencil sketch provides information quicker than an *information sketch* done in paint. On the other hand, you can get more from an *atmosphere sketch* done in color than in pencil.

Sketching habits are personal. You have your own requirements and restrictions. Your circumstances and methods dictate your sketching trips.

Always carry a sketchbook and pencil with you, especially when you go on vacation.

The drawing below is an information sketch, 16-1/2x11-1/2", done with a 2B pencil. The photographs on the opposite page show me working at the scene. The drawing at the top of the page is another sheet of the same size in my sketchbook. I sketched as much as I could. The old barge at the top of the sketch is the first exercise you will do. I have painted this barge many times in different moods.

The most important consideration for outdoor sketching, other than materials, is clothing. You must be comfortable and warm in cold weather. When you sit still for a few hours, even in mild weather, you can get cold. Take more clothing than you think you need.

You may want a folding stool or chair. It is not always possible to find an ideal place to sit and paint, such as a harbor wall or beach. You must be comfortable when you work.

The next problem is to decide what to sketch. I

Pencil information sketch, 16-1/2x11-1/2".

Pencil information sketch, 16-1/2x11-1/2".

have learned the following lesson from experience. When you find a scene, you say to yourself, "That's for me," or "Would it be better on the other side of that blue boat?" You walk to that spot, hesitate again, and walk to the next spot. You may waste all your sketching time looking for the best spot. This searching is not wrong. It shows enthusiasm, but it does not get work on paper. This has happened to me many times. Although I soak up the atmosphere, I have nothing to show for it.

Discipline yourself to draw or paint the *first scene* that inspires you. Then walk around and find the next one.

When you choose the scene, it can be difficult to decide how to place it on your paper. An excellent way to do this is to cut a mask or frame out of paper or thin cardboard. Make an opening about 6x4", as illustrated in the sketch at the bottom of page 40. Make the shape the same proportion as your sketchbook. Hold your hand up at arm's length and

Below is my photograph of the scene shown in the sketch on the opposite page. At right, I am shown sketching.

close one eye. Move your hand backward, forward and side-to-side, until the scene looks right in the opening. Note where the scene's main features hit the edges of the mask. Draw these key features in your sketch.

Sketching materials are determined by your medium. Pencil, pastel and watercolor equipment are easier to carry than equipment for oils or acrylics. If you know you will paint near your car, carrying equipment is no problem. If you are going to roam looking for a spot, then you should take only a limited amount of gear.

To do a day's oil painting with an easel and all necessary equipment, find a spot *before* you set out with your portable studio. Even the lightest equipment gets heavy, especially on a beach. Wrap your sketchbook in plastic. There is usually too much water around.

If you are not accustomed to sketching outside, start by pencil sketching. All you need is an HB and a 2B or 3B pencil. Sharpen them as I have shown in the photograph at top right. Leave a long, gradual taper to the lead so you can see the pencil point easily when you work.

I have shaded with HB, 2B and 6B pencils to show different tones. HB is the hardest pencil (light tones) and 6B is the softest (dark tones).

All sizes of sketching pads are available. With one or two pencils, a sketchbook and a kneaded eraser, you are ready to sketch.

Watercolor is the most convenient medium for painting outdoors. The equipment is easy to carry. You need a watercolor box, a watercolor sketchbook or sheets of plain writing paper, watercolor brushes Nos. 6 and 10, and a water container. An easel is optional. I don't use one for watercolor unless I am working on a painting larger than 20x15''.

One problem with watercolor is its unpredictability. Unforeseen things sometimes happen. You can save a watercolor if it gets out of hand and you don't have time to start again. Mix white opaque watercolor with your transparent watercolors to make them opaque. Go over areas you don't like and correct them.

An alternative is to turn the watercolor into a pen-and-wash drawing. Draw over your painting with a pen. Use black waterproof drawing ink, a felt-tip pen or a fountain pen. This can save a poor watercolor and make it a good painting. I have done this on many occasions.

Remember, your model does not come home with you! When you leave the harbor, all your information must be in your sketch unless you are using a camera. If necessary, put notes on your pencil sketches. Do not put notes on watercolor sketches, because these are often framed and hung as paintings. The more watercolor sketching you do, the more your sketches become finished works in their own right. You can still use them as information sketches.

For sketching, oils and acrylics require equipment that is harder to carry around. If you plan to paint in one spot most of the day, you only have to carry equipment to the spot. You shouldn't walk around with a lot of equipment looking for spots, setting everything up for an hour, and moving on again. It becomes tiring. You lose the fun and enjoyment.

Make sketching a pleasant experience. Enjoy the satisfaction of creating something, and gather information to work from later.

This is a mask, or frame, to help you select and compose the scene you wish to draw.

Right: These sketches are half their actual size.

This is the location, above, from which I chose to paint **Three Boats.** Below is my photograph of the scene.

When you sketch boats and harbors, pay attention to some common-sense do's and don'ts. Don't get caught by an incoming tide. If you are not sure about tides, ask. You may start work and find the tide moves so fast you must move before you are finished. It can be dangerous. If you sketch in a busy harbor, make sure you are not in anybody's way. Ask permission to work anywhere that looks private. If you are going to paint near an estuary, take your rubber boots. You will probably need them.

Below: **Three Boats,** 22x15-1/2''. This watercolor information sketch took three hours to complete. It is the type of sketch I often consider a finished painting.

Above: **Brixham Harbour, Devon,** 21x14-1/2". I did not use a pen for details in this watercolor information sketch. I am happy with the result, although I first thought I needed a pen.

Photograph of the scene at Brixham Harbour.

Detail from the painting **Brixham Harbour, Devon.**

Pencil Sketching on Location

In the following pages, I take six subjects and work each through stages for you to follow and copy. I give you a brush-by-brush account of how I worked on each subject. It is impossible to discuss *every* brushstroke, but I analyze each stage and explain important features and how to paint them.

Each stage is photographed to enable you to see the *same painting* in various stages of development. You can compare any stage with earlier ones.

The actual size of each painting is given so you can make adjustments to your own exercise. The size is printed next to the final stage. The close-up details of each exercise are actual size so you can see brush or pencil strokes.

I paint these subjects in my style, which has evolved over the years. The way I paint in this book is the way I habitually work. All painters have a personal creative style. This comes naturally. Once you master the medium, let your own style evolve.

In the first exercise, I re-create a normal routine—going on location, doing an information sketch in pencil and working from the sketch at home.

We work from this sketch in watercolor in the next exercise. I photographed the old, idle barge to show you what artistic license I took with the sketch and the watercolor.

First Stage—Sketch the distant hills, the old barge and the mud line below the barge on paper with a 2B pencil. Draw the shape of the barge, but don't put in details.

Second Stage—Work on the barge. Shade to create shadows and form. Start at the top and work down to the hull. Practice shading with your 2B pencil on scraps of paper. Get used to the tonal range of the pencil as shown on page 40. Put in the edge of the reeds, working your pencil up and down in dark and light strokes. Draw the rails on the barge and some details.

Final Stage—Work on the wet mud. Shade in the reflection and add details to the barge and the rest of the sketch. I have sketched this boat several times. Page 39 shows my sketch made on location. The character of the boat, mud and water always excites me.

First stage

Second stage

Final stage
14x9''

Painting a Watercolor from a Pencil Sketch

Let's start painting! This is the first exercise in color. Don't be tense about using paint. This is natural. I feel the same way when I start a special painting. Relax and read each step. Understand it before you start. If you prefer another medium, start with another exercise.

In these exercises, the color you mix *into* is the one I mention *first*. Add the other colors—in smaller amounts—to the first one. The first color is usually the main color. White is often last unless it is the main color. Oil or acrylic paints are shown at the beginnings of some exercises. These are the main colors used in the painting.

Because you sketched the barge in the previous exercise, you are familiar with your first painting subject. This will help you. The barge painting is on 140-pound, cold-pressed watercolor paper.

First Stage—Draw the picture with your HB pencil. Wet the paper from the top down to the barge with your No. 10 sable brush. Mix cerulean blue and alizarin crimson with plenty of water and work down the sky. Add yellow ochre and Hooker's green No. 1 to paint the hills and each side of the barge.

Second Stage—When the first stage is dry, paint the distant hills with your No. 10 sable brush and a mix of Payne's gray, alizarin crimson and yellow ochre. Work from left to right with horizontal brushstrokes. As you move down, add a little Hooker's green No. 1 to your colors. When the paint is nearly dry, add a wash of yellow ochre, alizarin crimson and a little Hooker's green No. 1 to show reeds. Let this wash overlap slightly with the last area you painted. This darkens the wash and gives depth.

Third Stage—Make sure the paint around the barge is dry. Paint the cabin with your No. 6 sable brush and alizarin crimson, yellow ochre and a touch of ultramarine blue. Paint both sides of the cabin, leaving two holes for the windows. Work around the rails, leaving paper showing. Use a weak wash of yellow ochre to paint the deck to the bow. Paint the open, dark area in front of the cabin, where there isn't any deck, with Payne's gray and yellow ochre. Use the same colors for the rails and shadow behind the cabin.

Paint the hull. Start from the stern and work along the light area with a mix of yellow ochre, alizarin crimson and a little Payne's gray. Use plenty of water, except for the rusty parts, to keep most of this area white. Paint the next section of the barge with Payne's gray, yellow ochre and alizarin crimson. Darken under the stern by using less water with your colors. Suggest the tops of reeds in front of the barge with downward brushstrokes. Use the same colors, with less water, for the darkest part of the hull.

Paint to the reeds as you did in the previous section of the barge. Put a shadow on the right side of the cabin. Paint a wash of ultramarine blue and alizarin crimson over the first wash. Don't forget to leave the windows and rails. Suggest trees in the background with a mixture of ultramarine blue, cadmium yellow pale and alizarin crimson. Use vertical brushstrokes, as you did with your pencil in the last exercise. To make areas darker, use more paint and less water. Make areas lighter by using less paint and more water. The reeds under the bow of the boat are darker because they are in shadow.

First stage

Second stage

Third stage

Fourth stage

Fourth Stage—Paint the mud and water. Don't copy my painting exactly, but use my method. The nature of watercolor makes each painting different. Use a No. 10 sable brush saturated in clean water for all the mud and water. Drag it over the area. Don't let the brush go everywhere. You are not trying to soak the paper, so keep some dry. You will have so-called "accidents" where paint runs into wet areas and mixes. This is desirable. Let the wet brushstrokes follow the direction of the mud, in perspective. Paint the reflected blue water with cerulean blue and clean water. Paint the mud and water with cerulean blue, Payne's gray, alizarin crimson, yellow ochre and Hooker's green No. 1. Work in broad strokes. Change your color mix as you go. Paint over the reeds on the right side of the boat to add shadow. When this is nearly dry, put in the barge reflection with your No. 6 sable brush and a wash of Payne's gray, alizarin crimson and yellow ochre. Use a wash of the same colors for the barge shadow on the mud and the reeds to its right.

Final Stage—By this stage you have various colors on your palette. Some are light, some dark and some in-between. Select an appropriate color to add details and crispness to your painting. Start with the barge. Use your No. 6 sable brush and a dark color to paint the cabin windows. Draw the planks on the shadow-side of the cabin with the brush point. Paint the rails and ropes with a dark mix of Payne's gray, alizarin crimson and yellow ochre. Paint a shadow wash over the dark part of the hull. Darken the mud

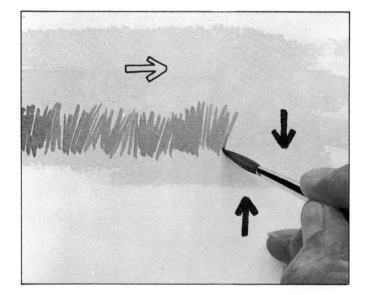

Final stage 14x9″

and reeds on the right to create shadows. Use the original dark hull colors. Use the same colors to darken reflections. Paint some lines on the mud with a strong color. Do not overwork a watercolor. Look at the fourth stage. It almost makes a pleasing watercolor as is.

Painting a Fishing Boat in Oils

First stage

Second stage

Third stage

I saw this fishing boat waiting to dock on a river. It was late evening and a misty, watery sun was going down. I used a gel medium to make the oil paint dry quicker on the oil-primed canvas. I sketched the boat on location and completed the painting in one sitting.

As is my style, I avoided overpainting. I didn't use a palette knife. I used the same brushes to mix colors and paint. I used a half-and-half mix of turpentine and linseed oil as my paint-mixing medium, and turpentine to clean my brushes.

First Stage—Draw the picture with an HB pencil. Using a No. 10 bristle brush, paint the sun area with cadmium yellow, yellow ochre, titanium white and a little alizarin crimson. Work from the center out. Add cobalt blue to your mix. Work down the canvas with the same colors, using horizontal brushstrokes for water.

Second Stage—Paint the distant hills, using your No. 4 bristle brush and cobalt blue, alizarin crimson, yellow ochre and titanium white. Start with the farthest hill and work toward the houses on the water's edge. Let the brush "wander around." Dab the canvas with light and dark colors, suggesting boats in the distance. Use the same colors to suggest boats to the right of the fishing boat.

Third Stage—With your No. 6 sable brush, put in the masts of the fishing boat with yellow ochre and touches of alizarin crimson and titanium white. Use the turpentine and linseed-oil mix to dilute your paint and make it run off the brush easily. For the rigging, use your No. 1 sable and ox brush. Paint the cabin with your No. 4 bristle brush and titanium white, yellow ochre and a touch of alizarin crimson. Add a little cobalt blue for the shadow areas. Put in details with your No. 6 sable brush. Use a dark color inside the hull and in front and back of the cabin. Change to a No. 4 bristle brush and cobalt blue, alizarin crimson and yellow ochre to paint the dark band around the top of the hull. Paint the main part of the hull with cobalt blue and touches of alizarin crimson and titanium white. Finish with the dark waterline band.

Final Stage—Put in reflections of the large fishing boat with a No. 4 bristle brush. Use the boat colors and horizontal brushstrokes. Paint the men with a

Final stage   12x16″

No. 6 sable brush. Use cadmium red and a touch of yellow ochre for the red one, and dark colors for the other two. Paint their reflections. Paint reflected light among the dark reflections with a No. 4 bristle brush and light sky colors. This makes the water more "watery." Don't be afraid to use thick paint for these highlights. Put in details you think necessary.

Sky and sea

Fishing boat

Cadmium yellow
Titanium white
Cobalt blue
Yellow ochre
Alizarin crimson

Painting Barges in Watercolor and Pen

Most artists who like painting boats get excited about old barges. They have character and distinction with their dark hulls and brown sails. Their numerous rigging lines for masts and sails can be difficult for a beginning painter, so this exercise is in watercolor and pen. The pen may help you suggest the rigging better than a brush.

Watercolor and pen is a natural technique for painting boats with masts, sails and rigging. I use a fountain pen and black India drawing ink. A felt-tip pen, a mapping pen or a sharpened matchstick dipped in drawing ink work just as well. The aim is not to draw every rigging line perfectly and in exactly the right place. Instead, try for atmosphere and feeling with a free-but-controlled brush and pen. The rigging may not be correct, but the impression is. Your aim in this exercise is the *impression* of two barges moored on a wet, muddy estuary.

First Stage—I used 140-pound, cold-pressed watercolor paper. Draw the picture with your HB pencil. Wet the paper with clean water, except for

the sails and hulls of the two main barges. Use your No. 10 sable brush. Load the brush with ultramarine blue, alizarin crimson, yellow ochre and plenty of water. Paint from the top, subtly changing your color mix as you descend to the bottom of your picture. Leave the horizon to the right of the barges unpainted. This clear area gives a distant look to your picture. Let the paint dry before you continue.

Second Stage—Paint the masts on the two foreground barges with a mix of yellow ochre and alizarin crimson, using your No. 6 sable brush. Paint the hull of the nearest barge with Payne's gray, alizarin crimson and a touch of yellow ochre. Lighten your colors by using more water and less paint for the end of the barge. Leave white paper to suggest lettering and a line across the stern. Don't paint the leeboard—the rudderlike device on the side of the barge. Use cadmium red with a little burnt umber for the red area. Paint it while the dark area is still wet to allow the colors to run together. Leave white paper for the mooring rope. Now, paint the more distant barge in the foreground. Use cerulean blue for the barge's blue area and the rowboat. Use the hull colors from the first barge for the dark areas. Use Payne's gray and yellow ochre for the white rowboat's shadow area. Leave white paper for the lightest areas. Strengthen these colors to paint the shadow inside the rowboat. Use cadmium yellow pale and alizarin crimson for the sails on the barges, adding Payne's gray for darker areas.

Third Stage—Paint the distant trees on the right with your No. 6 sable brush and a mix of ultramarine blue, alizarin crimson and yellow ochre. Leave white paper for the barge masts. Start on the left, loading your brush with plenty of water. Strengthen your paint as you work toward the right. Use the same colors for the trees on the left. Give the impression of trees with downward strokes. Wet the mud area below the barge with clean water. Paint the reflections with your No. 10 sable brush. Use the barge colors, but add a little Hooker's green No. 1. Continue into reflections of the sails, using the original sail colors. You are working on a wet area, so your colors will run to give a watery effect. You will not be able to duplicate the reflections I painted.

First stage

Second stage

Third stage

Fourth stage

Your water reflections will be unique. Paint the lee-board on the side of the hull. Use the hull colors, only lighter, and your No. 6 sable brush. Use the same colors and brush to paint the inside of the white rowboat again and the dark area of the blue rowboat. Paint over the hull with the same colors to darken it. Paint the deck, suggesting an impression of bits and pieces. Put in some rigging lines and their reflections.

Fourth Stage—Paint the hulls of distant barges with your No. 6 sable brush and a wash of ultramarine blue, alizarin crimson and yellow ochre. Use horizontal brushstrokes. Paint the mast and sails with a watery mix of the sail colors from the nearest barges. Use these colors to put in reflections on the mud. Paint the rowboat at far right with cadmium red and cadmium yellow pale. Suggest the boats on the left of the large barge with ultramarine blue,

alizarin crimson and yellow ochre. Put a darker line of these colors at the bottom of the trees on the left. Use Payne's gray and yellow ochre to darken the inside of the rowboat on the right. Darken the sails of the nearest barge, repeating the original colors with less water. Put a dark wash over the hull of the nearest barge and on the mud, so the boat merges with the mud. Use yellow ochre on the white part of the first barge's stern, on the mooring rope and on some rigging lines.

Final Stage—This stage is done with a pen and black drawing ink. Start on the nearest barge. Draw over the masts, sails and rigging. Work down the hull. Decide how many details you want to put in. Work the entire painting with your pen. Use my painting as a guide. Let the pen work freely, but don't labor the process. Create an impression, not an exact drawing of a barge.

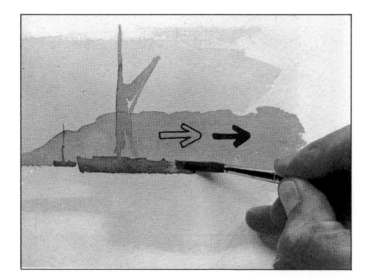

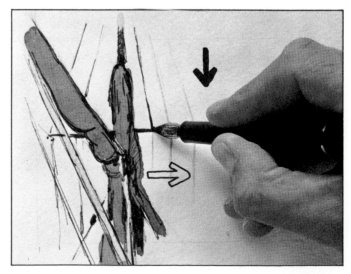

Final stage

21x14''

Painting a Ship in Acrylics

First stage

Second stage

Third stage

I like this subject. The *Queen Elizabeth 2* ocean liner is majestic, gracefully gliding into harbor as tugs rush around and tend to her. This is painted on acrylic-primed canvas.

First Stage—Draw the picture with your HB pencil. Put in the sky with your No. 12 nylon brush and cerulean blue, crimson, cadmium yellow and white. Start at the top and work down. Darken the colors as you approach the horizon. Use white and touches of crimson and cadmium yellow for high, fluffy clouds. Dab your brush across the sky to get this effect. Paint the light clouds to the right of the ship with a stronger mix of white, crimson and cadmium yellow.

Second Stage—Paint the distant hills and harbor wall with your No. 2 nylon brush and cerulean blue, crimson, cadmium yellow, bright green and white. Change colors and tones as you work from the top of the hills to the water's edge. Don't put in too many details. Paint the sea with your No. 6 nylon brush, using sky colors. The ship has left some water still and oily looking. Paint this with wet, downward strokes, as shown on page 24. Paint the

rest of the water up to this area with short, sharp horizontal strokes. Keep changing the colors.

Third Stage—Paint the ship with your No. 4 nylon brush. Paint the funnel. Work down the left shadow side of the superstructure. Don't put in details. Use sky colors for the shadow side and primarily white for the sunlit side. Paint the blue area of the hull with ultramarine blue, crimson, cadmium yellow and a little white. Use cadmium red for the waterline.

Now put in windows and dark shadow lines on the ship. Use No. 6 sable and No. 2 nylon brushes and a mix of ultramarine blue and crimson. Keep your paint watery. Paint the dark part of the funnel with the blue hull colors. Paint the tugs the same way. Use your No. 2 nylon brush. Paint the shadow side of the white areas, then the sunlit side and the dark hull. Note there are no specific details. Paint the tugs on the left darker because they are not in sunlight. Paint a dark reflection under the ship with your No. 6 sable brush. Use the hull colors, plenty of water and no white. With these colors, paint water movement lines from the tugs and the ship.

Final stage   12x16''

Final Stage—Put in remaining details with your No. 6 sable brush. Start with the mast and work over the ship. Use light and dark colors to paint boats in the distance. Put in white broken waves with thick white and a little cadmium yellow.

Sky and sea

White
Cerulean blue
Crimson
Cadmium yellow

Ship hull

Ultramarine
Crimson
Cadmium yellow
White

Painting a Harbor Ferry in Acrylics

This is a ferry I sketched a few years ago on acrylic-primed canvas. The day was chilly. I painted a passing rainshower to create atmosphere.

First Stage—Draw the scene with your HB pencil. Paint the sky with your No. 12 nylon brush and ultramarine blue, crimson, raw umber and plenty of white. Use less white for darker clouds. Go over the light area to suggest dark clouds breaking away from the main cloud area. Work down into the darker area, adding a little raw sienna. Put in sunlit clouds to the right of the dark ones using white, cadmium yellow and crimson.

Second Stage—Paint the distant cranes with your No. 6 sable brush and a watery mix of ultramarine blue and crimson. Paint the roof of the long shed on the left with your No. 2 nylon brush and white, plus touches of cerulean blue and cadmium yellow. Paint the brick buildings with crimson, cadmium yellow and a little white. Use cerulean blue, cadmium yellow and plenty of white for the warship to the right of the ferry. Put in the masts to the right of the ferry's funnel with your No. 1 sable and ox brush, using thin, watery paint. Add details to the buildings with light and dark colors.

Third Stage—To paint the water, use your No. 6 nylon brush and the sky colors. Work down the canvas from the distant buildings. Use plenty of white at first. Add more color as you proceed. Use horizontal brushstrokes. Paint the oily water in the foreground with downward strokes. Use the watery treatment illustrated on page 24. Show reflected sunlight to the right of the ferry with white and cadmium yellow.

Fourth Stage—The ferry is the center of interest. Paint the mast with your No. 6 sable brush and a mix of ultramarine blue, crimson and a little cadmium yellow. Paint the funnel with your No. 2 nylon brush and cerulean blue, cadmium yellow and white. Paint the cabin under the funnel with white and a touch of cadmium yellow on the sunny side. Add a little ultramarine blue and crimson, and use less white on the shadow side. When dry, use the mast colors to put in the door on the side of the cabin. Use the mast colors for the underside of the canopy. Paint the two boxes on the sides of the funnel with cadmium red and cadmium yellow. Put in the figures on the boat with your No. 6 sable brush. First, paint heads with cadmium red, cadmium yellow and white. Work down from the heads. Use colors to suit the mood of your painting. Paint in downward strokes. If the figure faces away from you, indicate hair, but in some cases leave a little neck showing. To paint a profile, put a dark color on top of the face for hair or a cap. Carry brushstrokes down for the clothed body. When painted with freedom and confidence, these *suggested* figures add the right touch. Paint the dark areas left of the cabin and under the life preservers with a No. 2 nylon

Sky and water

White
Ultramarine
Crimson
Raw umber
Raw sienna
Cadmium yellow

Green of ferry

White
Cerulean blue
Cadmium yellow

Dark hull of ferry

Ultramarine
Crimson
Burnt umber
White

First stage

Second stage

Third stage

Fourth stage

brush and ultramarine blue, crimson and burnt umber. Leave the rails unpainted. Paint the life preservers with cadmium red and a touch of raw umber. Use a bluish white for the white sections. Next, paint the hull with a No. 2 nylon brush. Paint the top edge with ultramarine blue, crimson, burnt umber and a touch of white. Start at the stern and work toward the bow. Clean your brush and use the funnel colors for the blue-green band around the ferry. Add more cerulean blue on the shadow side. Continue with the dark hull underneath this band. Show a reflected highlight on the stern with a little white. Paint reflections with your No. 6 nylon brush and a watery wash of ultramarine blue, crimson and burnt umber. Work in downward strokes, but let the brush go sideways at the edges to show movement. I used two washes to get the proper darkness in the reflection.

Final Stage—Mix the colors you used earlier for water and add more white. Use your No. 4 nylon brush to work the water into the reflection with short, horizontal strokes. Work the lighter water colors from side-to-side over the reflection. Imagine the water. Feel it move and swirl as you paint. Let the brush jump and move around as if it were in water. Put highlights on the people in the ferry. Paint the canopy supports, rails and rigging with your No. 1 sable and ox brush. Use ultramarine blue, crimson and a touch of cadmium yellow. Add plenty of white for the lighter areas. Show the canopy edge with white and a little raw umber. Put darks and lights on the harbor buildings. Paint the yachts left of the ferry. Add more highlights to the water to the right of the boats and to the edge of the dark clouds above the funnel. Paint a whiff of smoke from the funnel. Look at your painting later with a fresh perspective. Add highlights and darks as you think necessary.

Painting a Fishing Village in Pen and Pastel

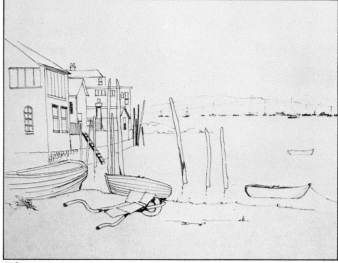

First stage

Second stage

I originally painted this scene in watercolor. The poles in the foreground and next to the house are for drying fishing nets or laundry. The tide goes down and you can walk out to them without wearing waders. It is a good watercolor subject because the poles contrast against the light water. I decided to try it again in pen with pastel over it, using my watercolor painting as an information sketch. I used a pen with black India ink and worked on 140-pound, hot-pressed watercolor paper.

First Stage—Draw the picture in HB pencil. This gives you confidence when you redraw it with pen and ink. Don't put details in with pencil. Draw over the buildings on the left with pen. Add the poles, boats and distant hills. Work on the foreground boats and handcart. Don't try to copy pencil lines exactly with the pen. Use them as a guide. Don't draw perfect penlines. Work the pen freely, even if you draw two or three lines instead of one. This gives character to the drawing.

Second Stage—Use your No. 6 sable brush and black ink diluted with water. Mix ink on a palette or saucer—don't put water into your ink bottle. Use watery ink on the background. Paint the rocks in the middle-distance. Carry one brushstroke from the rocks to the right across the water. Work on the trees, houses and poles. Create different tones by adding water to your ink. Use undiluted ink for

Third stage

most of the foreground and under the two rowboats on the left. Finish with free, horizontal brushstrokes on the beach. Move the brush up and down, leaving white paper to suggest stones.

Third Stage—With pastels, work from left to right on the distant hills, using sap green and green-gray. Add burnt umber and smudge these colors together in places. Next, paint the buildings. Use yellow ochre for light yellow areas and burnt umber for brown areas. Add cadmium red for the roofs. For

Final stage 19x14''

the pink house, put a little roof color on and rub it in with your finger. Paint the seawall under the houses with green-gray. Merge it into some houses above with your finger. For the side of the nearest house, use burnt umber. Paint over it with green-gray. Apply the pastel lightly where you want the ink wash to show. Rub it with your finger if you want a smooth effect. You create another pastel tone when the background shows through. Use cobalt blue for the nearest windows. Put in the reflections. Paint the middle-distance rocks with burnt umber and green-gray. Rub these in with your finger.

Final Stage—Paint the poles with burnt umber, sap green and green-gray. Paint the boat on the left with burnt umber. Use cobalt blue for the blue boat and sap green for the bottom. Paint the white boat with yellow ochre. Use all your pastels except cadmium red and cobalt blue for the beach. Paint it with long, horizontal strokes. Rub and merge colors with your

fingers. Use these colors for the handcart. If you overdo the pastel or want to take some off your painting, remove it with a kneaded eraser or bristle brush. Add crispness and details with your pen. Draw the ropes around the net poles in pen.

Points to Remember

- Buy the best materials you can afford.
- Don't use acrylic paint over oils.
- Be observant. This is the key to good painting.
- Convey the mood of your painting in the sky.
- Always paint water horizontally.
- Keep details simple while you are learning.
- When necessary, use photographs as aids.
- Don't worry too much about technical details.
- Vary the amounts of color used in a mixture.
- Relax. Keep practicing.

Glossary

Amidships—In the middle of a boat.

Beam—Width of a boat at its widest part.

Boom—Horizontal spar that holds the bottom of the mainsail.

Bow—Front of a boat.

Hull—Lower portion of a boat, the part that floats on water.

Jib—Triangular sail stretching forward from the mast.

Leeboard—Rudderlike device attached to the side of a flat-bottomed boat. It is lowered to control the boat's leeward drift.

Leeward—Direction in which the wind blows.

Mainsail—Large sail set on the main mast.

Mast—Vertical pole for supporting the sails.

Port—Left side of a boat when facing forward.

Rigging—All the ropes and lines of a boat.

Rudder—Underwater steering device near the stern.

Sheet—Line or rope used to adjust a sail.

Starboard—The right side of a boat when facing forward.

Stays—Mast supports—usually wire.

Stern—Back of a boat.

Index

7.3265498642